the living arts of Nigeria

Edited by William Fagg   Photographs by Peccinotti   Illustrated by Michael Foreman

the living arts of Nigeria

72- 172828

The Macmillan Company, New York, New York

Editorial consultant: Walter K. Wilson

Copyright © 1971 by Omnific

The Macmillan Company
866 Third Avenue, New York, N.Y. 10022

Designed and produced by Omnific Design Limited

Library of Congress Catalog Card Number: 72-77278

First American Edition 1972

Printed in England

The Editor acknowledges with gratitude the contributions made by the following organizations and persons: the management of Mobil Nigeria for translating their interest in Nigeria's cultural heritage into the opportunity for making this work possible; to Dr. Saburi O. Biobaku, Vice-Chancellor of the University of Lagos and Chairman of the Antiquities Commission of Nigeria, for his interest and counsel at each stage in the book's development; to Mr. Ekpo O. Eyo, Director of Antiquities, Nigeria, and his staff, for making available the resources of the Nigerian Museum, Lagos, and for guidance and advice as the project evolved; to the Trustees of the British Museum for kindly allowing photography in their collections; and, not least, to the artists and craftsmen of Nigeria, for the large part unnamed, whose talents and skills are depicted in this record. *W.B.F.*

Foreword

All will agree that the art of a people is the outward and visible symbol of their culture and civilisation. Too often, however, do we conceive this in terms of magnificent pieces displayed and occasionally studied in national museums or ensconced away and continually admired in the private collections of the affluent. We link art generally with the past and in Nigeria the well-known Nok heads and figurines, the Ife terra cottas and Benin bronzes provide incomparable examples of the artistic excellence once attained by the peoples of Nigeria. But there is more to art than that.

Art is the manifestation of the undying soul of a people. It is an aspect of their genius which is manifest in the great works no less than in the day-to-day utensils which they use, the cloth they wear and the ornaments with which they adorn themselves. In all these and more, real artistic merit can be discerned and recognised. *The Living Arts of Nigeria* has done this precisely for us. Through exquisite and accomplished photographs and drawings, and with the authoritative introduction by William Fagg, the arts of Nigeria have been brought into focus and placed in their true perspective as living and continuous processes of the people. We can not only see the artifacts but we also gain an insight into the actual processes which give rise to them as well as view at work the people who conceive and execute them.

As Professor of African Studies in the University of Lagos, I acclaim this superb contribution by the Publisher and Mobil to our understanding of the culture of the peoples of Nigeria. As Chairman of the Antiquities Commission of Nigeria, I commend this book to all who wish to have a deeper understanding of that culture and evaluate as well as appreciate the artistic excellence attained and currently maintained by the Nigerian people.

Saburi O. Biobaku
Vice-Chancellor
University of Lagos

Introduction

This book is an account of an extraordinary and unprecedented *tour de force* – a 14-day expedition by four people innocent of anthropological or ethnological knowledge or training, but equipped with powers of observation (and material equipment) worthy of the best journalism, and charged with doing a reporting job on the state of traditional crafts in Nigeria. Never before has an enterprise of this kind been undertaken for any part of Africa. For one or two countries – all too few – there have been ethnological descriptions of tribal crafts, carried out over a long period, but never with such resources of brilliant photography and draughtsmanship. The expedition members, after a briefing at the Nigerian Museum on some of the places to visit, performed prodigies of recording, making hundreds of photographs and many drawings, of which only a selection can appear in this book, many others being omitted only with the greatest regret. To this nest of eagles, then, I am appointed the straight man.

This is not, needless to say, to be thought of as a textbook, still less as an encyclopaedia. Rather is it a sampling of the very many crafts of Nigeria, chosen because they still flourish, though mostly in greater or less degree now dependent on overseas tourists. Furthermore, it is exoteric and impressionistic, being intended primarily to interest the general public. Yet ethnologists or ethnographers may learn from it too, especially if they have sometimes thought of doing a compendious work on the technology of one country: let them form a team with a first-class professional photographer and if possible an artist, and with suitable planning the job should be done in less than a month's work. There is room for at least one such book for each of the African countries and for many others in the rest of the world.

A few years ago (in *Nigerian Images*, 1963, p. 19) I wrote some sentences on Nigeria's archaeological riches which have been much quoted since. 'When the contributions of all other African countries are added together, they indeed illumine certain by-ways of artistic history, but in Nigeria alone can we discern the main stream of artistic development through two millennia and more. Of all the known works of African sculpture to which we can safely attribute an age of more than a century, probably at least nine-tenths are Nigerian; moreover, this remarkable pre-ponderance seems continually to increase as more and more antiquities come to our knowledge on and under the Nigerian soil . . . Unless some fortunate chance should bring unsuspected sculptural riches to light elsewhere in West or Central Africa, it is to Nigeria that all the African nations must look as the principal trustee of the more durable fruits of the Negro artistic genius.' It occurs to me now to ask myself how far this estimate of the riches of the Nigerian past may be applicable to those of the present. It is not to be expected that any preponderance should be anything like as great in Nigeria's favour as ninety per cent., for, if that estimate be accepted, and it now seems to me rather an under-estimate than otherwise, it results from 2500 years' accumulation of sculpture in durable materials, which was practised especially in the Nigerian area; other regions of West Africa may have been just as rich in perishable materials. If we confine ourselves to the tribal crafts in all materials of, say, the past century, the balance must necessarily be very greatly redressed, since it might show excessive partisanship to suggest that Nigerians are *per capita* more artistic than the peoples of Ivory Coast and Ghana, Gaboon and Zaire. Even on this basis Nigeria, with two or three times the population of any other African country, might be expected to show a correspondingly richer heritage of traditions of craftsmanship. Yet even this does not, I think, sufficiently account for the immense variety found there, and in part at least suggested by the selection shown in this book; and if this impression is correct, it may be due to the fact that Nigeria contains something like a quarter to a third of all the tribes of Africa, and also to its position at the 'fulcrum' of Africa, as a result of which it would no doubt benefit from the many currents of diffusion of culture which have passed through it over the millennia. (The crucial event of the African Neolithic, the discovery or introduction of food-production, superseding food-collecting, seems to have taken place in the border areas of northern Nigeria and Cameroon, whence it – and all the consequential developments of settled culture – spread through Africa.)

Margaret Trowell, in her admirable textbook *African Design* (second edition, 1966) – each of the chapters of which could, and should, be expanded into a whole volume – summarizes for us the traditional decorative crafts of all Africa south of the Sahara. Almost without exception these crafts and techniques can be found within Nigeria (although her own examples of Nigerian crafts are drawn from only eight of some two hundred tribes) and it will be convenient to use her chapter headings and their subdivisions as a framework for a brief survey of the almost unlimited field for further study there.

The first group of design techniques is entitled Wall Decorations (including rock art). It is divided into: naturalistic mural painting; abstract design in mural painting; naturalistic low-relief panels in clay, wood and metal; abstract design in moulded relief; painted and moulded ornament on the surface of walls and ceilings; decorative reed work. All these are found in Nigeria, and we may note in passing that although rock art is not a particularly important art tradition there, the Margi in the north-east have the distinction of being the only African tribe still practising it, in intimate association with initiation rites and with rock gongs (an ancient form of musical instrument in which Nigeria is particularly rich).

The next chapter is devoted to Pattern on Mats and Screens, subdivided into: woven mats; sewn mats; plaited mats – all present in Nigeria.

Textile Design is divided into: woven cloth; embroidered cloth; patchwork; appliqué; painted cloth; dyed cloth, tie dyeing; dyed cloth, resist method. There are only two categories – printed cloth, and dyed cloth, the discharge method – for which I cannot remember a Nigerian example.

Ornamental Basketry yields: woven basketry; coiled basketry; baskets showing variation in materials or texture. Nigeria is especially rich in all forms of basketry.

In Beadwork Nigeria has some of the finest and most highly developed traditions in Africa.

The Decoration of Hides and Leather has the following categories, all found in Nigeria: shaven pattern; pattern carved in low relief; appliqué work on raw hide; painted hide shields; decoration of tanned leather; *tandu* work, an amazingly ingenious method of making vessels by stretching animal gut or inner skin over clay forms to dry, then pulverising the clay by beating the vessel from the outside. (The best bindings for European books are in 'morocco', which is Nigerian goat skin, so called because it has been imported into Europe for the past two or three centuries by way of Morocco.)

Cicatrization and Body Painting are (or were) very highly developed in Nigeria. Europeans have a rather unreasonable prejudice against the ornamental use of scar tissue, and the attendant infliction of pain, usually in moderation, but once this prejudice has been overcome, there is a whole other world of artistry to admire.

Calabash Patterns are divided into: carved pattern; scraped pattern; scorched pattern; engraved pattern; decoration with extraneous materials; carved coconuts (a related technique). Nigeria is infinitely the richest country in the world in calabash decoration.

Decoration on Wood divides into: texture pattern; representational forms in carved design; black and white woodcarving; painted pattern on wood; scorched pattern on wood; decoration of wood with extraneous materials. All of these are found in Nigeria.

So, in unsurpassed richness, is Ornamental Ivory-Carving, a material which lends itself to the finest flights of Nigerian decorative virtuosity.

Decorative Metal Work has two principle forms: beaten metal design; cast metal design. In both these Nigeria is of course pre-eminent.

Lastly, Pottery Design in Mrs Trowell's classification comprises: impressed pattern; incised pattern; moulded pattern; coloured or burnished decoration; encased pots (in which the casing is generally of basketry). The only category (not strictly pottery) which is probably not found in Nigeria is cow dung bowls (known from the Nuba Hills in the Sudan).

But the recital of this catalogue – hardly exhaustive though it is of the technological resources of the tribes of Nigeria – cannot begin to suggest the richness of the spectrum. For this there would be needed, first, a further catalogue, for each of these categories, of the tribes among whom it occurs, and these are in most cases many; and second – and only at this stage would the said richness begin to show itself forth – the illustrative documentation of all the differing tribal styles of craftsmanship in each technological category, and, even more important, of the astonishing variety of design adopted by localities and individuals within each tribal style.

The British Museum has played a leading part in breaking down, since the Second World War, the old-fashioned *idée reçue* that there are no individual artists in African tribal sculpture. But I cannot claim the *discovery* that all tribal artists have identifiable styles, and that some of them are as great in relation to the mass of artists as are the great masters of Europe; a few scholars had previously acknowledged an individual master as transcending tribal style (as Frans Olbrechts had acknowledged the Master or Masters of Buli in the Republic of Zaïre), but this often seemed rather like proving the rule by an exception. But when I first went to Nigeria in 1949, before there was a Nigerian Museum, I had the immense benefit of collaborating, when I first worked on the Yoruba, with the first Surveyor of Antiquities, Kenneth Murray, and learning, both from him at first hand and by being given full access to the archives in which he had set down, on typewritten cards with photographs, the results of twenty years' work in southern Nigeria, the fact that the 'rule' was 100 per cent. wrong. (Can there be another case where the main research archives of a national museum, as they still are, and indeed some of the collections also, were in existence many years before the museum was founded?) In the field, armed with his data on named artists, I immediately found it easy to identify more pieces by the same artists, and then new artists, good, bad and indifferent (for even

the worst do not sink into that undifferentiated mass, the 'anonymous tribal artist'). Such identifications have since become standard practice in fieldwork in Nigeria, and when, later, Adriaan Gerbrands found the same to be true in Western New Guinea (*Wow-Ipits*, The Hague and Paris, 1967), there was little excuse for ethnographers anywhere in the world not to enquire the artist's name when collecting or photographing in the field a work of tribal art.

The preceding paragraph is by way of being a preamble to a perhaps more surprising claim, which I do not think has been made before as of general application, that in tribal crafts as in tribal sculpture it is possible (though somewhat harder) in most cases to distinguish the hands of the individual craftsmen and craftswomen. In 1950 among the Bakuba in the Belgian Congo (now Zaïre), I found it fairly easy to detect the hand of Pierre Pongo, an excellent traditional itinerant carver of finely decorated boxes for camwood powder, who lived near Port Franqui and travelled around the Bakele subtribe about his business (like the other Bakuba carvers, he was also able to carve inferior tourist art for the Belgians without any visible effects upon his purely traditional work for the Bakele – a phenomenon for which I have no parallel in Africa). Yoruba *adire* dyeing provides an excellent illustration of individualism, many designs being peculiar to one woman dyer, while others show differences of treatment in different hands. Although I have done no work on identification of *adire* at the centres of production, I did collect one highly complex piece of tie dyeing which I found in three different towns, Abeokuta (where it was said to have been made), Ilorin and Ife; all were quite clearly by the same woman, and the complication of the technique showed such virtuosity that analysis has baffled the skill of many textile experts to whom I have shown it, in spite of their initial confidence. The men weavers of narrow-width cloth are almost certainly able to recognize their own work, even though the designs are from a local repertoire of named patterns, and if they can do so, so also can the student. (There are said to be men in the British wool trade who from a glance at a man's suit can say from which of several hundred woollen mills the cloth came; one such was A. R. Baines, the Wool Controller during the Second World War. This of course is mass production, and does not involve identifying the work of individuals, but the degree of detective skill is similar.)

Only where there is great emphasis on uniformity, as with the spherical pots of the Adarawa Hausa of Sokoto and Kano, are the works of individuals not likely to be recognizable – this indeed is incipient mass production. But if there is a reasonable element of truth in my claim, that the study of tribal crafts as well as sculpture should be personalized, then its mere enunciation should be enough to cause ethnographers and others to review their experience and produce the evidence. This book, by its constant emphasis on the artist-craftsman, is an ideal one for the purpose of making the point. *William Fagg.*

the living arts of Nigeria

On beads and beadwork

'Beads!' was one of the ideas most readily evoked by the word 'Africa' in the callow European, reared on stories of African adventure in the good old days of Queen Victoria (which, for this purpose, lingered on until the Second World War). The picture was of the pioneer trekking through the bush at the head of a long line of bearers with many a headload of trade beads, obtained very cheaply at home, but much more highly prized by the Natives. (He must have felt the need of market research as he found that beads which were acceptable in one tribe were anathema to the next.) Descendants of our callow European now travel freely to Africa, returning often with loads of trade beads, not invariably recognized as such.

The true picture of beads in the history of Africa, though often obscure, is somewhat different. They are no doubt as old in Africa as anywhere else in the world, and we may take it for granted that beads of perishable materials were being made in Africa (as they still are) long ages before their first appearance in the archaeological record. In Nigeria, stone beads of many shapes and sizes, and even probably some made of tin, were used in the first of the 'artistic' cultures – the Nok culture of the first millennium BC. By the ninth century AD, the grave goods of the minor divine kings of Nri in the western Ibo country at Igbo-Ukwu seem to have included many thousands of stone and glass beads of rather uniform shape, often used imaginatively in association with bronze sculptures of extraordinary rococo-like detail (though it is not quite established that the beads are contemporary with the bronzes on which they occur). But probably the apogee of the bead-making art in Nigeria came at Ife in Yorubaland a century or two later, even though we can judge the beauty of the finest Ife beads far better from the fine crucibles, whole or fragmentary, which are dug up in the Olokun grove, with glass in beautiful shades of deep red and blue, turquoise and several shades of green, than from the actual finished beads which survive to our time.

About beadwork, or beads in composition, there is both more and less to be said, for the permutations are almost infinite. But the peacock-like flamboyance of the beadwork worn by the Yoruba Obas when in state, which is the most striking manifestation of the bead in Nigeria today, is an example of a whole new style of decoration founded on the importation from Europe of tiny beads of unlimited variety of colours. For there is evidence that until less than two centuries ago, Yoruba crowns – like those still in use at Benin – were made of much larger beads of red carnelian, agate, jasper and perhaps also (as at Benin) Balearic coral – all except the last of local origin. One of these older crowns is still kept in his mountain fastness by the Owa of Idanre. Since the right to wear beaded crowns is in the gift of the Oni of Ife, the most exalted of Yoruba rulers, it seems that the invention of the new style must have occurred nearby, and where more probably than in the Adeshina family of Efon-Alaye, who now purvey crowns to most of the crowned heads of Yorubaland?

Bida in the Nupe country, north of the Niger, has for centuries been famous for beadmaking and indeed for making glass which is mainly used for armlets. Nowadays they produce almost entirely for the tourist, and no longer make their own glass, but melt down and recycle the glass débris of civilization. So the modern expert must be able to recognize Guinness, Star and other beer bottles, Fanta, Seven-Up, Coca-Cola, Ponds Cold Cream and Mentholatum from a glance at a necklace. The technique of working the glass remains, however, very much as before, and the workshop is visually indistinguishable from that painted by Arriens on the Frobenius Expedition in 1910–11.

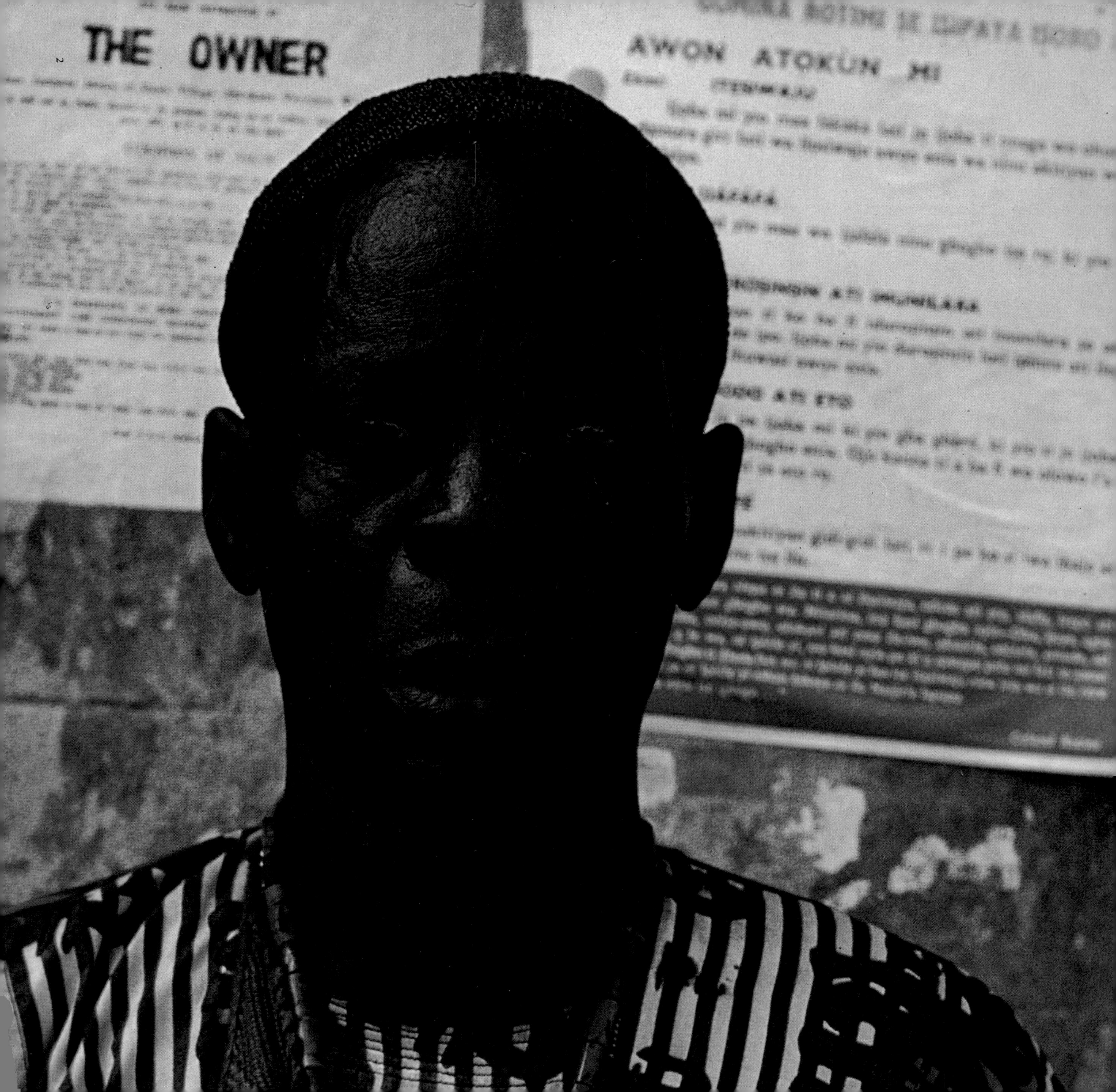
THE OWNER
AWON ATOKUN

One man keeps the fire red hot by pumping the bellows: he holds a stick in each hand and pushes and pulls at great speed making a thump, thump, thump sound like incredible drumming. He keeps up this rythm the whole time the other fellows make the beads and bracelets.

3

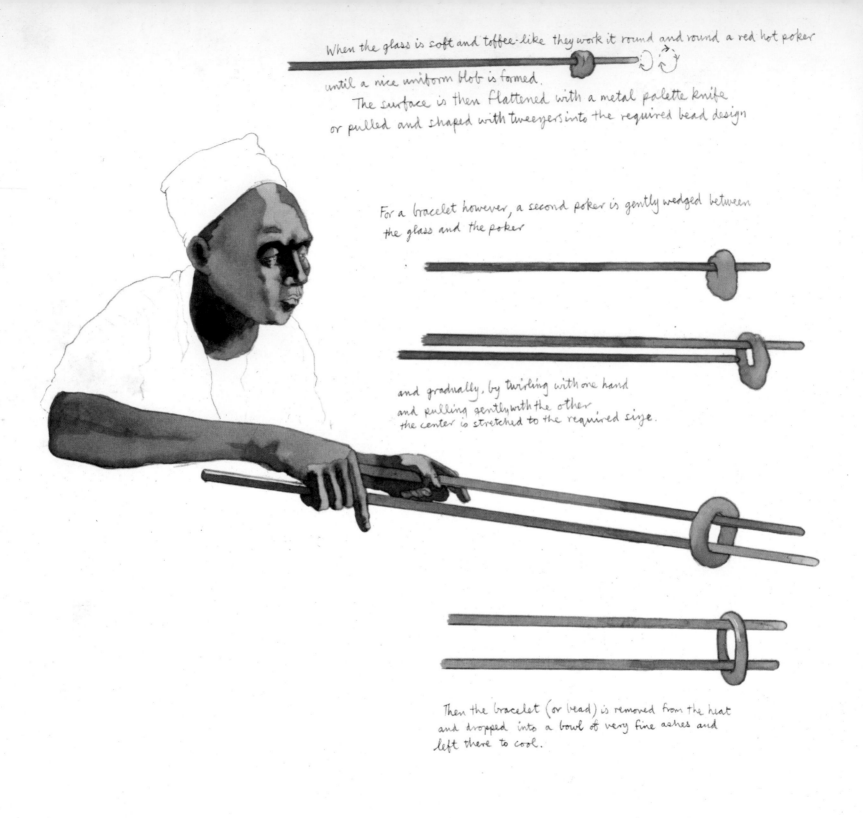

When the glass is soft and toffee-like they work it round and round a red hot poker

until a nice uniform blob is formed.
The surface is then flattened with a metal palette knife
or pulled and shaped with tweezers into the required bead design

For a bracelet however, a second poker is gently wedged between
the glass and the poker

and gradually, by twirling with one hand
and pulling gently with the other
the center is stretched to the required size.

Then the bracelet (or bead) is removed from the heat
and dropped into a bowl of very fine ashes and
left there to cool.

Plate 1: Assorted beads from various Nigerian markets.

Plate 2: Samuel Adeniyi Kenke, maker of crowns, with one made for His Highness Oba Samuel Adesina Gbadebo II, the Alake of Abeokuta, of whose death we learn with regret while this book is in the press. Kenke may be affiliated to the Adeshina family of crown-makers at Efon-Alaye, forty miles east of Ife; he stays in the Alake's palace while making crowns for him.

Plate 3: In the beadmaker's workshop at Bida in the North-West State – relieved by characteristic Nupe triangular windows – the craftsmen apply ancient methods to modern materials for modern markets. The bellows are of the old West African type of bowl bellows, shared with ancient Egypt, as opposed to the more modern bag bellows (made of two complete goatskins fitted direct to the nozzles), which are increasingly diffusing from modern Egypt and the Republic of Sudan through West Africa. Both types are commonly 'played' as though they were drums.

On brass-casting and brass-working

There is a rough and ready convention by which all alloys of copper – from pure copper through tin-bronzes to zinc-and-lead brasses – are loosely described as bronzes if they are antique (or provided that they are accepted as fine art, of whatever age they may be up to the present), and as brasses if they are not. So Benin works from before the British Expedition of 1897 are commonly called bronzes, even though most of them are strictly brasses, while those dating from after this climacteric only qualify as brasses (except of course when masquerading as 'bronzes').

Of the two main ways of processing brass, by casting and by working and beating, Nigeria is pre-eminent in Africa in the first (though not so pre-eminent as she once was in the casting of 'bronze') and surpassed only by the North African countries in the second. Both are carried on by the old methods, with little modification.

Benin is still the greatest centre of brass casting, and almost all the work done there is made for sale to visitors. The casting is done by members of the hereditary guild of brass-casters, the *Iguneromwon*, headed by two principal chiefs, a senior, Chief Ineniguneromwon, and a junior, Chief Ihamaniguneromwon, more familiarly known as Ine and Ihama. Since commissions from the Benin chiefs have virtually dried up, they rely entirely now upon sales to tourists and to local Bini dealers or entrepreneurs, many of whom turn the honest revivalist art produced by the craftsmen into fake antiques by applying chemical and other techniques to age them. These fakes all date from 1958 or later; since then it is likely that the number made exceeds the total number of genuine Benin bronzes. After 1958, when the eyes of the entrepreneurs were opened to the ways of the world, many of them decided to cut out the members of the guild and try their own hands at the mystery of brass-casting, with variable success: often, when they had a casting failure, they did not throw it back to be remelted, but sold the defective piece as a primitive casting dating from a period when the craft was new to Benin. (Antiques are increasingly being made at some Yoruba centres, and the best of these are less easily detected, since there is no single corpus of genuine works to refer them to, as at Benin.)

The working or beating of sheet brass is concentrated in the Nupe capital of Bida, though also practised at various Hausa centres in the north. It is no doubt much more recent in Nigeria than brass-casting, having probably been imported by the Moslems from the Near East some centuries ago – perhaps in some kind of association with the peculiar method of pottery-making by beating found, as we shall see, at Kano and Sokoto. (We should note, however, that historically beating of non-ferrous metals precedes casting, since man at the transition from the stone to the metal age seems first to have treated native copper as just another stone with some peculiar properties.) Nowadays, the Bida industry makes mainly dishes and trays for the tourist, but before the First World War fine ewers and other elaborate vessels were made from brass sheet 'raised' on a yielding base to form hemispheres which were then tinned on the inside and fitted together.

Filing brasses after casting at the front of the compound of Chief, Ihama of Benin.

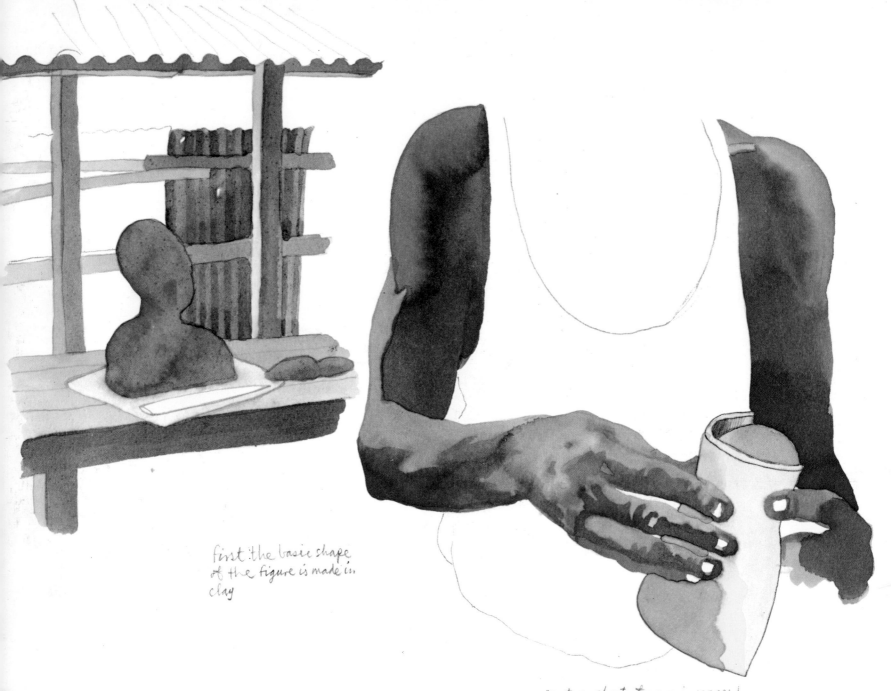

first the basic shape
of the figure is made in
clay

next a sheet of wax is wrapped
and modelled around the clay form

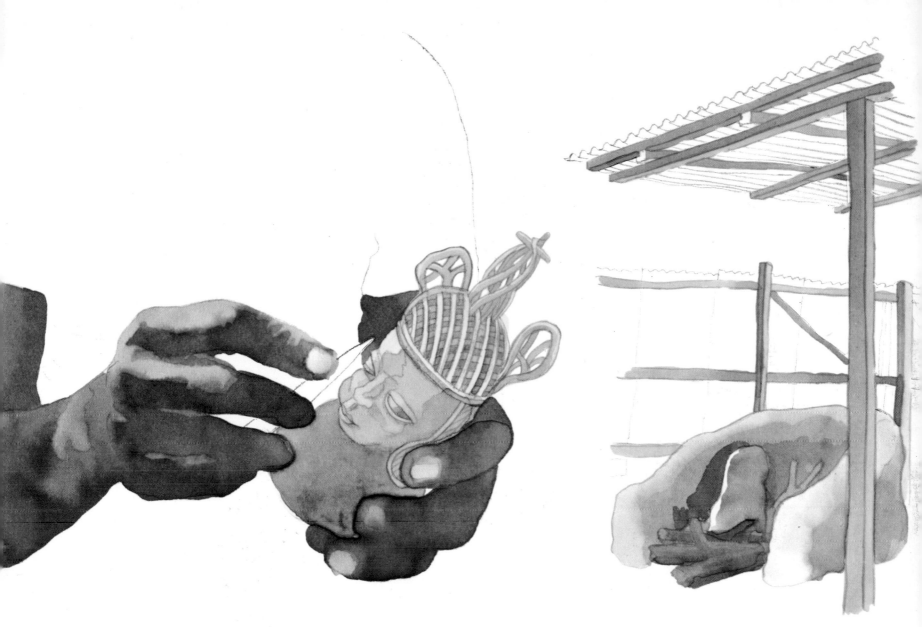

details are sculpted in and additional decorations
are applied in wax.

The model is covered with clay, and when
dry, is heated upside down over a small
fire to burn out the wax.

Brass is heated in a crucible
in the furnace with a large
imported bellows,

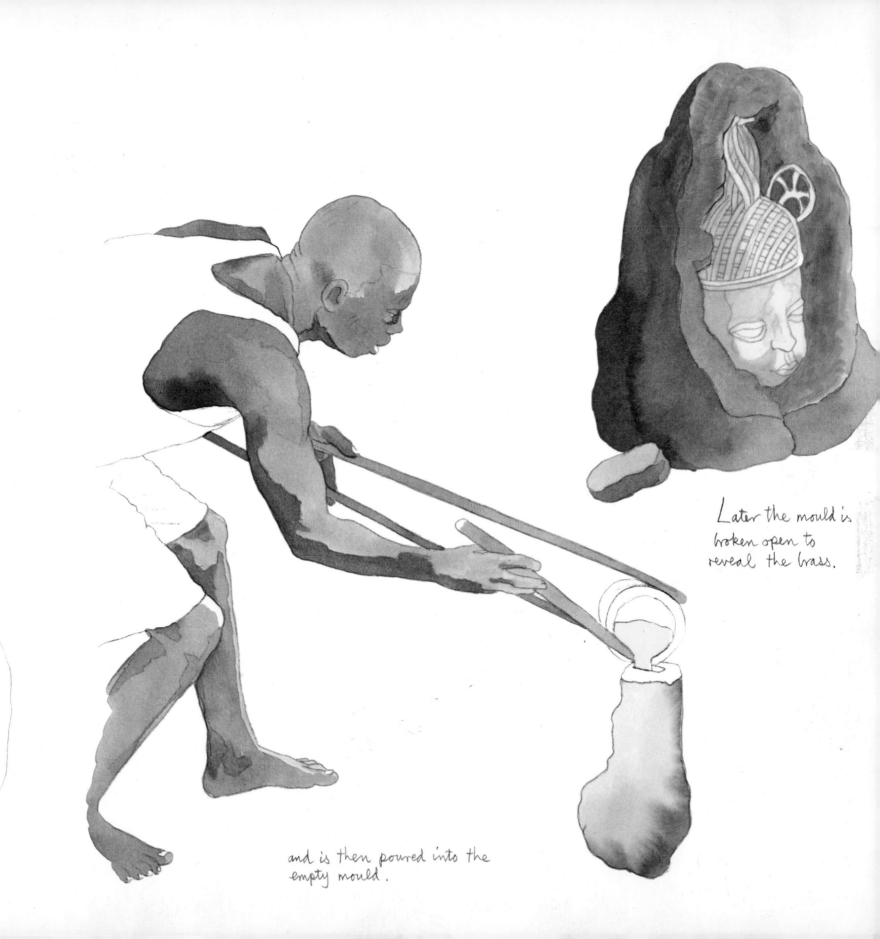

and is then poured into the
empty mould.

Later the mould is
broken open to
reveal the brass.

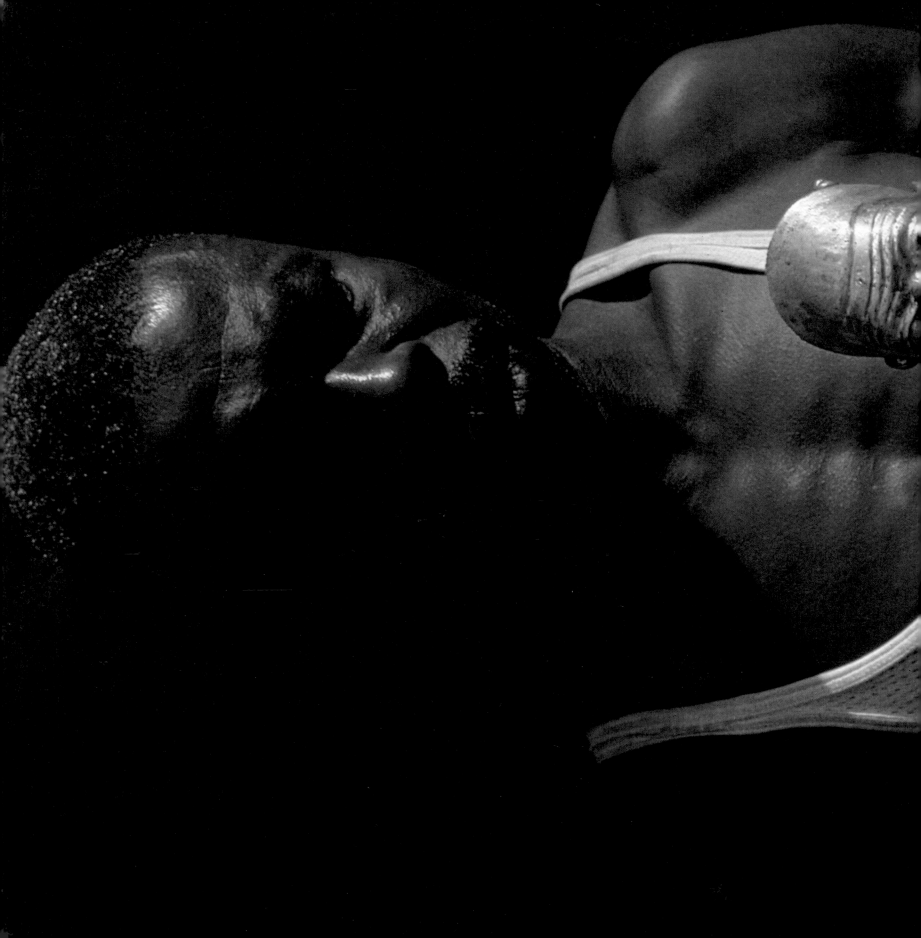

6

Plate 1 : In the workshop of Robinson Isere Ihama, son of the chief (his first name, after the amiable Benin custom, is that of a British District Officer at the time of his birth). One of the most popular subjects, a standing leopard, is seen as a finished sculpture in wax, now to be translated into brass by being first invested within a clay mould and then melted out and replaced by molten metal. The surface detail of these leopards is, by comparison with that of the old Benin bronzes, considerably exaggerated; but this did not prevent some of them, subsequently patinated, from changing hands as ancient works in the United States in the years following 1958.

Before the introduction of European files, the work had to be nearly perfect when it came from the mould, but nowadays the emphasis has shifted from casting to the final filing.

Plate 2 : Similar waxes partly invested with clay but still requiring at least one more coat (each coat is left to dry for a day or two) stand alongside part of the inner clay core of a human head in the foreground. These are also in Robinson Ihama's workshop.

Plate 3 : This skilful blend of African and European art is a representation of Oba Ovonramwen, deposed in 1897 after the Benin Expedition.

Plates 4 & 5 : Two fine old vessels of unusual shapes from the Nupe in the British Museum collection. According to Frobenius, who collected some pieces and studied them in 1910-11, many pieces of these types were two to three hundred years old.

Plate 6 : Two urns or ewers worked by the Nupe from brass sheet, and tinned inside to hold water. These are in the British Museum.

On dyeing

The dyeing of cloth is one Nigerian handicraft which is not 'other-oriented' but is done essentially for Nigerians and not for tourists; these may be glad enough to buy dyed cloths but do not provide a significant proportion of the demand. The trade is in a happier condition in the north, where there is little competition from imported textiles. The Yoruba, on the other hand, have long been enthusiasts for brightly coloured cloths from overseas, and there is only a minority demand, though fortunately a persistent one, for home-dyed cloths.

In the north, most big towns have a large open space where the dyepits are situated. Each dyer has several of these pits, each about eight feet deep, some for actual dyeing and one or two for rinsing. The unmistakable aroma of the indigo – nowadays used together with aniline indigo from Europe – lies over the place, for the dye is often allowed to accumulate and to become stale. (The reason why the Nigerians have not gone over entirely to aniline dye is because, being fast, it does not come off on the skin, a desired side effect.) The cloths are left lying full length in the potent mixture for a day or two, then rinsed and dried by being laid out on the surface. The pits are nowadays generally lined with cement, as in the Kano example pictured opposite; fortunately, we have contented ourselves with full colour, although full odour might have provided a useful exercise in a new publishing technique.

Anyone who has travelled even for a day in the north has seen chiefs and notables wearing deep blue shiny turbans loosely wound round their heads, and these give a wonderfully rich appearance to their attire. This gloss is not, however, a property of the cloth, but is imparted to it in the following manner. The cloth is first dyed indigo in several dippings until saturation point is reached; the indigo content is then still further increased by a technique similar to the much more ancient (in fact pre-textile) method of making barkcloth: the cloth is laid over a tree trunk and beaten vigorously with heavy mallets or beaters, liberal amounts of dry indigo in powdered form being sprinkled on it and becoming the main vehicle of the gloss (just like the kaolin filling of the coated art paper opposite).

The Yoruba are the finest practitioners of pattern-dyeing, which they call *adire*. There are several techniques, but all are based on the same principle of reservation of certain areas of the cloth from the dye, so that the pattern is seen in white or in lighter blue on the dark blue background. The reservation may be effected by tying up parts of the cloth with raffia, string or thread, or by tying small stones or seeds into it, or by the resist method, in which cassava starch is painted on to the cloth either freehand or through stencils (originally of leather, then of zinc, and nowadays of tin). The main centres of *adire* dyeing are at Abeokuta and Ibadan, but it is practised almost universally by the Yoruba wherever they are found, in the Yoruba colonies among the Hausa towns in the north and even along the West Coast as far as Sierra Leone and Senegal.

2

Limawua: a small village a few miles from Kano, where they did their own dyeing
  and also made some cloths shiny.
  In a small dark hut from which poured fantastic drumming rhythms,
sat a group of men pounding on a piece of dyed blue cloth that
was stretched out over a pole, so that section by section, they
beat it with wooden mallets until a very high gloss is obtained.

The effect is enhanced by sprinkling indigo
in powdered form on the cloth under the mallets.

This process is done to coarser fabrics.

Dyeing at Abeokuta

Material is bunched and bound
with wax coated string in the
traditional TIE DYE process.

Industrially printed fabrics are
often over printed in the villages
Here starch is being applied with
the use of stencils.

The actual dyeing is done in large pots with
corrugated iron draining boards.

Drying the fabrics after dyeing.
The ground beneath is dyed the
same colour as the fabric

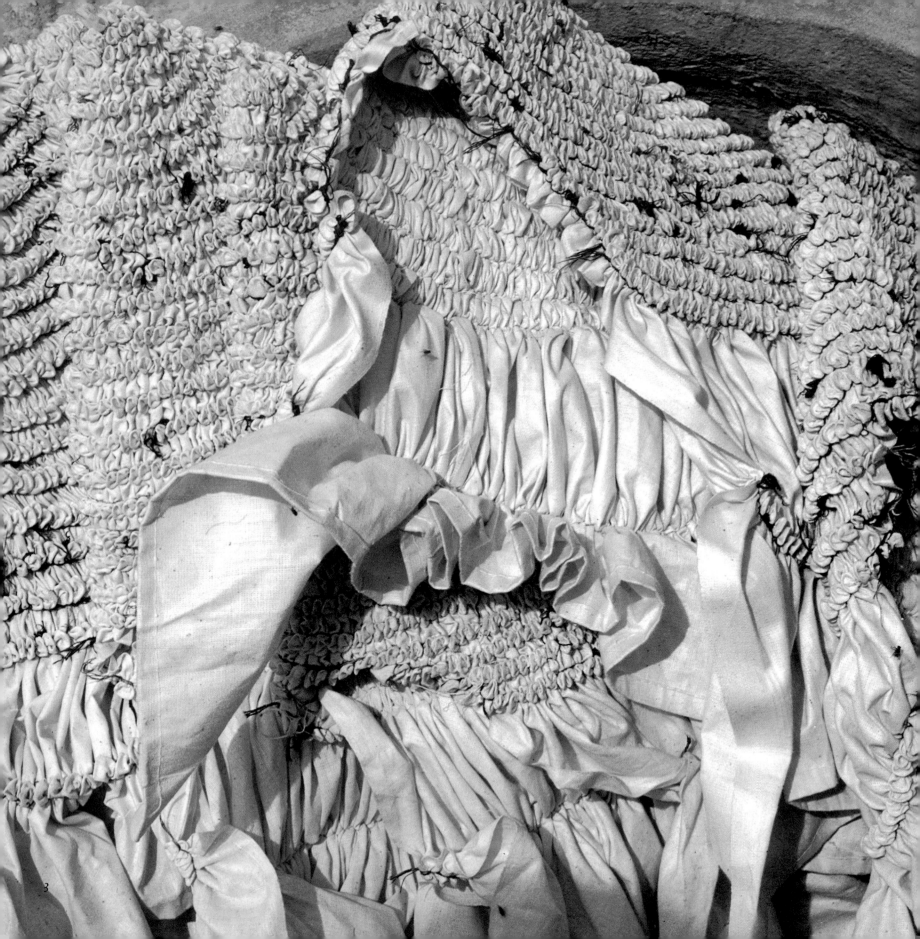

Plate 1: One of the dyepits at Kano seen in bird's eye view, showing the thick 'crust' which forms on top of the fermenting indigo (and provides a potential breeding ground for the anopheles mosquito). The pits are about $2\frac{1}{2}$ feet in diameter and eight feet deep.

Plate 2: General view the of dyepits at Kano, showing various stages of the dyeing process. Among the Hausa, dyeing is a male preserve, whereas among the Yoruba (whose equipment for the purpose is notably more compact) it is largely done by the women. Many of the men have their arms stained deep blue up to the elbows, but the custom of wearing rubber gloves is now becoming established.

Plate 3: A large imported white cloth prepared for dyeing at Kano, (probably by Yoruba women, perhaps married to Hausa). It is sewn up in such a way that when it has been dyed and then unpicked, the areas with which the thread is in contact will form concentric circles of wavy lines in white or paler blue on a ground of dark blue.

On leatherwork

As befits peoples whose culture is founded on the horse, the Hausa, Fulani, Tuareg and Kanuri of the northern States have carried to great heights the craft of leather-working. This is to be distinguished from the working of hide, which is untanned, and tends to be used by less sophisticated tribes. Fine leatherwork is one of the attributes of the great and fairly homogeneous Moslem culture which stretches from Senegal to northern Cameroon, taking in the Manding-speaking tribes as well as the Hausa (who are perhaps West Africa's most numerous people), two tribal groups whose artifacts are often so similar as to call for a special category, 'Hausa-Manding', for undocumented objects conjecturally identified in the study collections of the British Museum.

All four of these peoples overlap widely into neighbouring countries; only the Tuareg are not native to Nigeria but present only as frequent visitors to the northern fringes of the country. They are, of course, horsemen *par excellence* and it is not surprising that their leatherwork is among the most sought-after of all. They are not Negroes but Berbers, and the Fulani and Kanuri also have a Berber admixture. The Hausa, who were formerly pagan, and of various origins, acquired their homogeneous culture under the influence of their Fulani overlords in mediaeval times, in the period of Moslem expansion.

Leatherwork is not, however, confined to the northern states, though its most important manifestations in the south seem to owe much to connections with the north, even where it is found among pagan (or non-Islamic) groups such as the followers of the cult of Shango, the Yoruba god of thunder. This cult is found throughout Yorubaland (except at Ife) and its unity is preserved by, among other things, certain beautifully decorated leather pouches worn by the priests during ceremonies; their surprising uniformity was accounted for in 1949 when I discovered that they had all to be obtained from the Magba or high priest of Shango at Oyo, which before about 1830 was much farther north on what is now the border between the northern and southern states. Moreover, Shango had very strong connections with the Nupe of Bida, who are particularly fine leatherworkers.

At a Kano tannery skins are soaked in large cemented vats of tannic acid.

Scraping a skin on an old disused mortar.
These are normally used to hold grain when being
pounded.

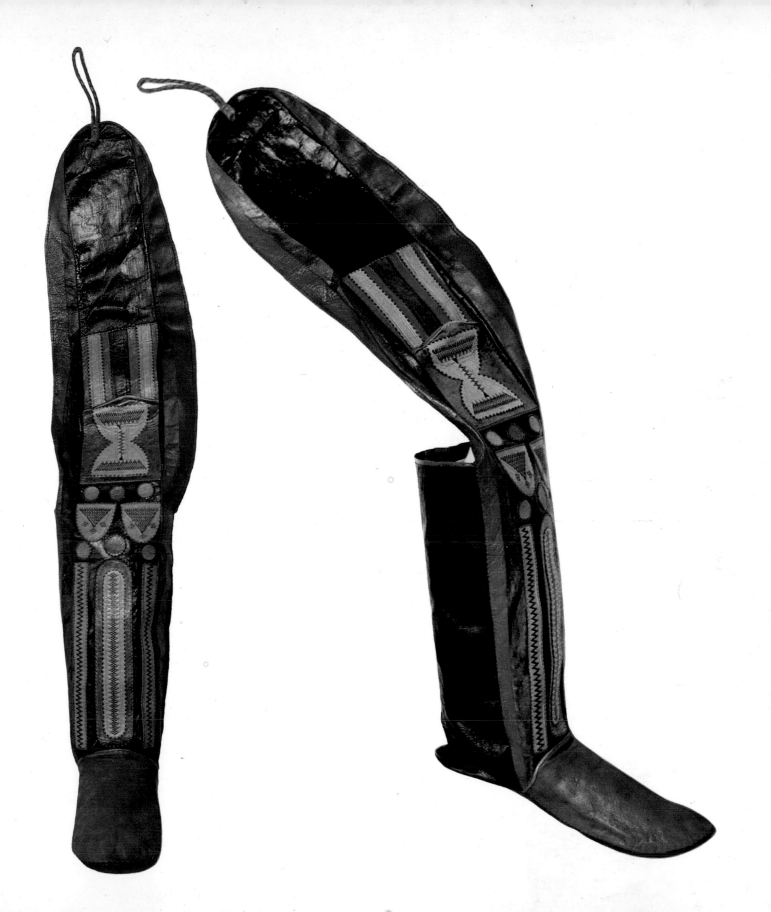

Making sandals at Kano, in close proximity to the abattoir and tannic acid vats.

4

Plate 1 : A leather pouch collected among the Hausa, from the British Museum. The beautiful appliqué and sewn work, however, is in the characteristic style of the Tuareg, from whom it must certainly have been obtained. Exactly similar bags may be found, for example, among the Ashanti of Ghana and the Dogon of Mali, and no doubt much farther afield.

Plates 2 & 3 : These magnificent leggings, in the British Museum, seem worthy of an Emir and must surely have been made for one of the most important of the Fulani aristocracy of Kano, where they were collected.

Plate 4 : Two fine pairs of new sandals, still sewn together sole-to-sole, collected for the British Museum among the Hausa in the mid nineteenth century. One, of enormous size, is decorated with a fine flourish of ostrich feathers.

On pottery-making

Scratch the surface of any Yoruba or Hausa town of two or three hundred years' standing or more and you are sure to find that it is built, like Troy, upon a great midden consisting almost entirely of potsherds, occasionally as much as twenty feet deep. Such a town, for example, is Ile-Ife or Ife, the most ancient spot in the Yoruba world, where the Creator sent down three gods and sixteen chickens to the surface of the primeval waters to scratch up the mud which formed the earth. Archaeology cannot yet confirm this story, but has already shown the town to have been inhabited for about 1,400 years, and the materialistic modern city, a great centre of the cocoa trade, overlies the débris of many millions of broken pots, varied occasionally by fine terra-cotta heads and figures and also by countless fine pavements made from trimmed potsherds set on edge; these can often be seen in the sides of the open drains of the town and show where chiefs' houses and shrines were in ancient times.

Nigerians are not likely for a long time to come to cease from laying down this detritus of their culture at their feet, for although enamel and plastic basins have become disfiguringly common, and are indeed more efficient for some purposes, it is probable that more traditional pots than ever before are being made, given the increase in the population. They are still remarkably cheap, so much so that they are regarded as expendable, and needless to say are much more beautiful, though it is probably more to the point to say that they are excellently adapted, through long trial and error, to the indigenous cooking methods and other purposes for which they are used.

Nigeria has an immense variety of traditions of pottery-making, a great many of them represented in the unique Pottery Museum at Jos, and recently published in Sylvia Leith-Ross's book *Nigerian Pottery*. In the vast majority of them the potters are women, practising variations of the coil-building technique (the commonest all over Africa) in which new clay is continuously added to form the walls and the mouth of the pot – though the 'coil' is really a four-dimensional one, less than half a coil being visible at any one time. Our illustrations, however, are mainly devoted to the peculiar technique practised by the Adarawa Hausa at Sokoto and Kano (and here studied at a village near Kano) in which the pot is 'raised' by beating from a depression in the ground – to use an expression drawn from the raising of metal bowls, with which this technique seems to have an affinity. The method produces near-spherical pots of an almost mechanical perfection, and the generating depression is formed by rotating an actual finished pot in the hollowed and moistened ground. It is difficult not to see some Arab or Middle Eastern influence in this highly ingenious technique, which has something in common with the wheel and the compass. It is practised chiefly by men.

We begin, however, with a picture of a more typical woman potter at Bida with a finished pot, in the building of which a sort of saucer or turntable (it might be the base of a broken pot) is used; not for the purpose of the potter's wheel, but merely for the convenience of the potter, who rotates it with her feet to avoid the necessity of walking around it. The true potter's wheel was not used in Africa south of the Sahara, but this was not through ignorance but from a positive aversion to it. In any case the two techniques – with and without the wheel – are fundamentally different and one could not evolve into the other.

He then takes a piece of clay, wets it, rubs it in the red powder, kneads it like dough, and hammers it into a plate shape, formed initially by the hollow he dug.

Gradually, hammering the clay all the time and smoothing with a wet cloth, and turning it in the hollow, he works it up into a circular pot. When it is the shape and size he wants he powders it again, flattens the rim with a palette knife and bends it over a little, making a thicker rim.

He wets the outside of the pot and makes a decoration around it with a twig. He draws a line with the palette knife above and below the pattern.

* Decorations vary with the mood of the potter. Sometimes nails or knotted strings are used.

Then he takes another piece of clay
of a paler colour and rolls
it into a sausage shape

This he works onto
the top of the
pot to form a
thick rim

He wets the rim and, using his foot, turns the
pot round and round smoothing the edges and
neck with a wet leaf. Finally smooths the pot
over all by gently rolling around the hollow he made.

Plate 1 : A potter at Bida, the Nupe capital, with an elaborate pot produced by the coil method with the help of a turntable which she rotates slowly with her foot.

Plate 2 : At the village of Dawaki near Kano a mass of sun-dried pots made by the peculiar method of the Adarawa Hausa are packed ready to receive the top covering of grass. A light is then set to it and the fire lasts for about half an hour, by which time the pots are finished – in one sense or the other, for African potters generally accept a high proportion of 'wasters'. Behind are piled up safely completed pots from a previous firing. Kilns are not used in sub-Saharan Africa (except in non-traditional potteries, such as that founded by the potter Michael Cardew at Abuja and its offshoot at the Jos Museum).

Plate 3 : Women at a well at Limawua, the next village to Dawaki, using spherical pots of the Adarawa Hausa type.

On weaving

Weaving with a loom must have been developed – probably at more than one place and time in human history – from simple mat and basket weaving without a loom, a laborious process by comparison. The ingenious principle involved – which though first invented, presumably, in the Neolithic age, was also to play a great part in the Industrial Revolution in eighteenth-century England – is the almost philosophical idea of the shed and the countershed, into which a set of warps or lengthwise threads are alternately divided (by the use of heddles which raise one half of them and then the other) to admit the creative penetration of the shuttle bearing the weft or crosswise threads. An infinity of variations and refinements on this basic idea have provided for the proliferation of woven-in patterns wherever art has been added to utility in the weaver's craft.

Weaving is another of the ancient crafts of Nigeria which are still carried on vigorously with little direct foreign influence (apart from some imported dyes and yarns) and, though much cloth is sold to Europeans and other visitors, this does not appear to have any perceptible deteriorative effect, since the pull of indigenous demand is many times stronger.

The customary division of labour into heavy and light along sexual lines is in operation in Nigerian weaving, the women using the broad loom, which is generally vertical, while the men work at the narrow-strip or ribbon loom, which is arranged horizontally in a light wooden frame and stretches for about thirty yards in front of the weaver. But although many tribes have both these methods in active use, it may not always have been so, for the men's loom seems to be a tradition of the interior, and the women's loom a tradition of the coastal tribes. It should be noted that the narrow strips woven by the men are then made up into cloth of full width by the women.

From Nigeria's textile riches, one broad-loom and one narrow-loom industry are here illustrated. At Akwete, where Iboland touches the Niger Delta, the Ibo women weave a characteristic style of cloth with some design elements worked in by embroidery in the course of weaving, somewhat in the manner of tapestry weaving. It seems that at some time they have had at least an infusion of style from the Yoruba women of Ijebu-Ode, another famous centre of the same type of decorated cloth: some techniques and some designs (like the anthropomorphic, or zoomorphic, example in two of our photographs) are shared, and some think that the whole industry was transplanted from there. Hausa expertise with the horizontal loom is represented by weavers at Limawua, who are typical of those found in most Hausa towns and, so far as technique goes, of most Yoruba towns as well.

Akwete cloth is made by the women of the village. Mothers teach daughters at an early age
and each house contains as many looms as there are females in the family. The beautiful little streets are
full of the rattle and click of looms.

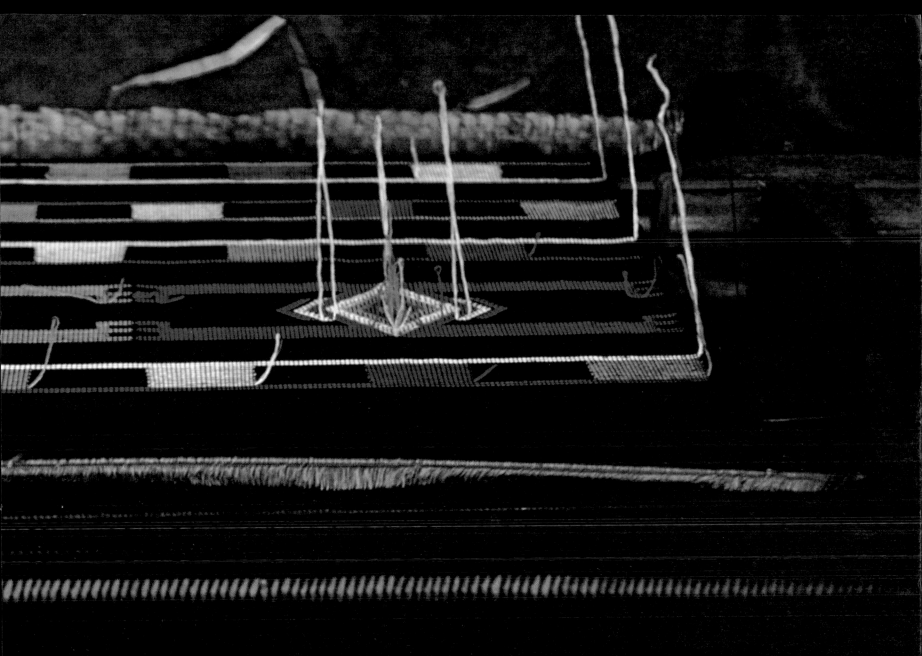

Laying the warps for mens narrow looms at Abeokuta.

Plate 1 : A new cloth photographed at Akwete at the eastern edge of the Niger Delta, in which the embroidery threads can be clearly distinguished.

Plate 2 : An old cloth from Akwete (collected by Sir Raymond Menendez, first Chief Justice of Nigeria, about 1905–8) bearing a design which may be interpreted as a human being or a crocodile or lizard; this is also found at Ijebu-Ode in south-east Yorubaland. Akwete cloths usually have a pronounced taper, due to an idiosyncratic practice of the weavers which causes the cloth to finish about two or three inches narrower than it began. This one is in the British Museum.

Plate 3 : An Akwete loom seen from above, with white, orange and red embroidery threads hanging from the cloth. This is a kind of puzzle picture : find the camera angle. The photographer, conscious of his virtuosity, insists that it is printed correctly, with the foot of the loom at the top of the picture. It seems to follow, gravity having the same force at Akwete as elsewhere, that the loose threads are hanging vertically and the loom itself is inclined at an angle – with the photographer leaning over the top of the loom frame from the back to shoot in towards his own feet. The cloth being woven is black (both warp and weft) and the pattern is essentially carried out in embroidery. The photograph is bisected horizontally by the heddles and the black area on the lower half of the pages (that is the upper part of the loom) consists of the warps which have not yet received the weft.

Plate 4 : Weaving at Limawva. The men work at great speed, although beating-in the picks of weft to make a firm cloth is very much lighter work on these narrow looms than on the heavy women's looms, where the 'sword' type of beater-in must be brought down with great force for each pick of weft. Careful examination of this picture will make clear the essentials of the narrow-loom technique.

Plate 5 : A detail of another new cloth seen at Akwete.

On wood-carving and calabash-decoration

Of all the tribal areas of the world – in which dynamism in sculpture flourishes, or used to flourish, as it never has done in the post-tribal areas – West Africa, and above all Nigeria, are pre-eminent. Yet in most places the traditional sculpture is now moribund and no method has been found of carrying it on in a way which will make it viable in the post-tribal world. (There are some prominent exceptions to this, notably the great old carver Bamgboye and the much younger Lamidi Fakeye, but they seem only to prove the rule.) In the detribalizing process, the tribal religion seems to be the first to be undermined, and sculpture, being fairly closely tied to it, soon fades out. As a result, the sculptors whose commissions have dried up revert to farming as a full-time occupation. Other forms of sculpture arise in the post-tribal situation, namely tourist art (mostly in ebony, as demanded by the Europeans), which bears little or no relation to the tribal art, and contemporary art, which is affiliated to the International Style. These are not quite what this book is about. (One cannot deny that the contemporary art is a 'living art', but it is not 'of' Nigeria in the sense of having roots in its past. In fact, by definition contemporary art is not supposed to have any roots.) So recourse has been had to the great riches of the Nigerian Museum and wood-carving has been represented here by a clutch of masks – the most viable of the tribal art forms because of their partly recreative function and their intimate connection with dancing – and some of these are chosen for their adaptation to modern life or their relevance to modern art.

It is a truism to say that there are many examples of Cubism – or something very like it – in African art, but masks are often a striking illustration of the breaking-up of surfaces into triangular and lozenge-shaped facets in order to catch the light as they move in the dance. (In fact, Cubism seems much more functional in this mobile sculpture than in modern painting.) The Ibo headdress of the Maiden Spirit is of this kind, though its Cubism is somewhat muted to show beauty (whereas it is exaggerated in the counterpart mask of the Elephant Spirit). The Gelede mask from the Yoruba which carries on its head an admirably

simplified (and rather early) motor car with passengers is an example of the readiness of this cult to adapt to the modern world, which has given it the durability to survive in Lagos itself until now. The long anthropo-zoomorphic mask from Epe is startlingly 'pop' in appearance; but a little research would probably establish that similar masks were known before Dada and Duchamp, let alone the recycled Duchamp of the sixties. It would be going too far to say that the origins of each of the schools of modern art are to be sought in Africa, but at least the Africans had a remarkable knack of anticipating them (sometimes by as much as 2500 years).

Two specimens of calabash-decoration, which could readily be expanded into a whole book, complete our sample. Although the Baikie specimen, of undetermined provenance, represents probably a now extinct tradition, calabashes are never likely to go unused in Nigeria, or to remain undecorated.

Adugbologe's house in the 'Brazilian' style at the sacred Olumo Rock at Abeokuta with his son Makinde at work indoors and apprentices nearby.

I

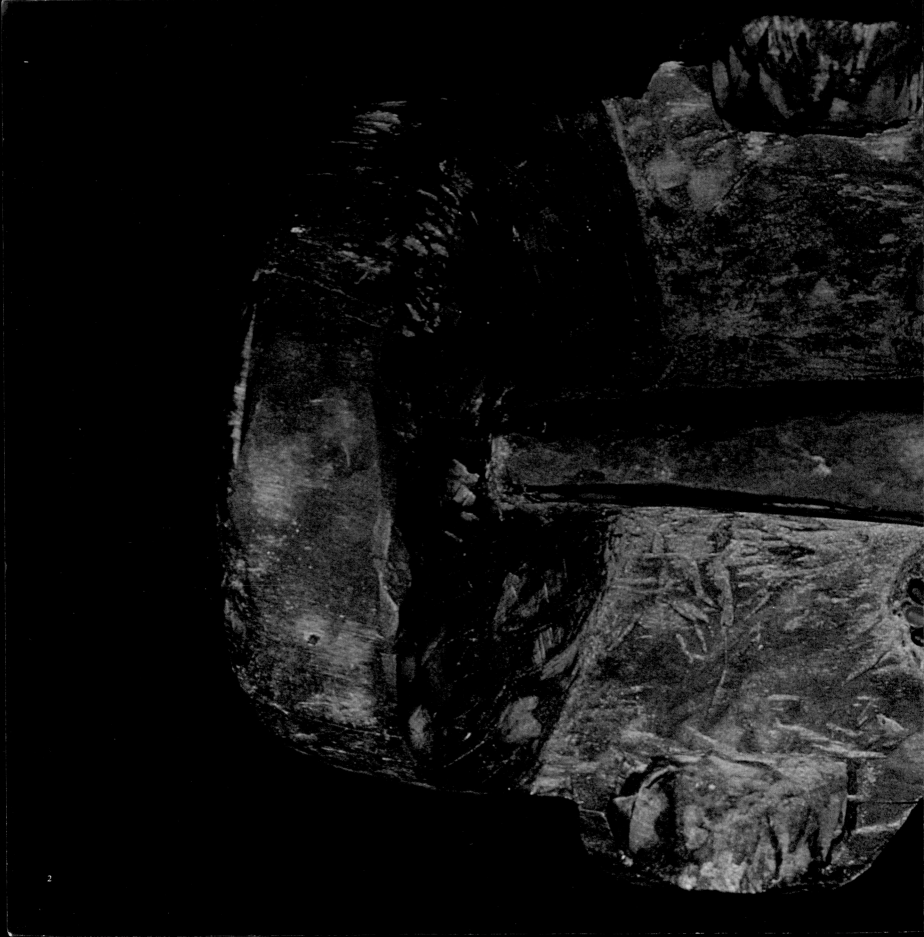

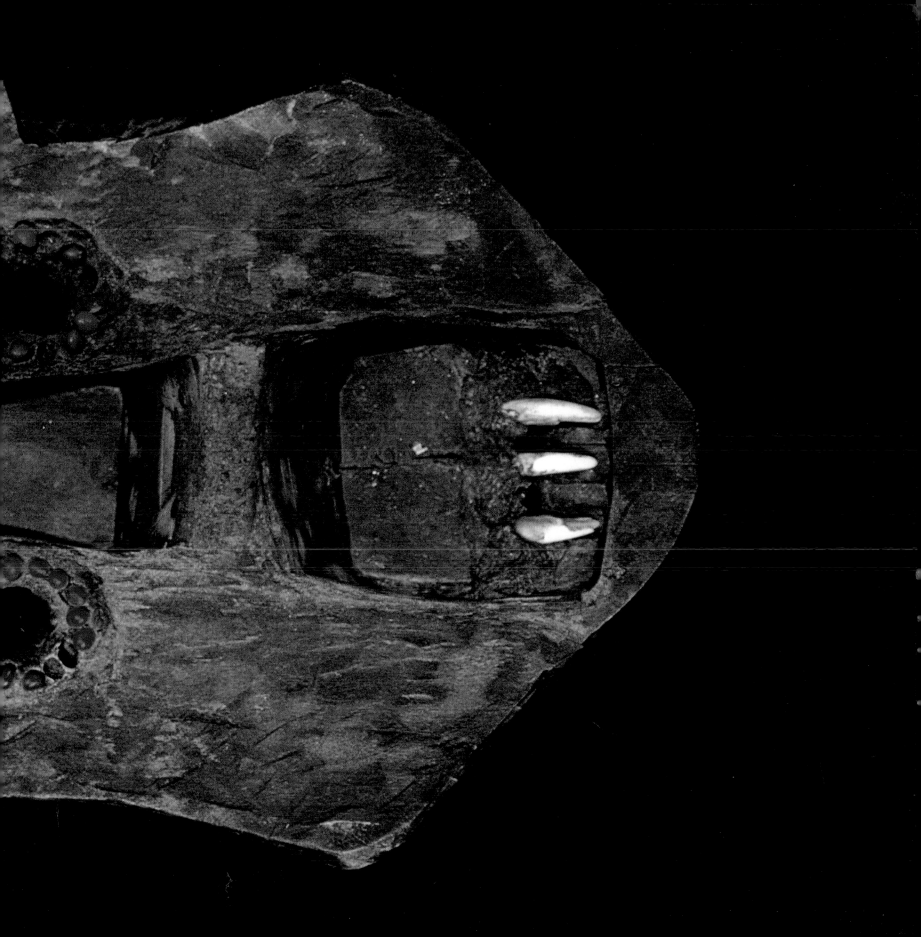

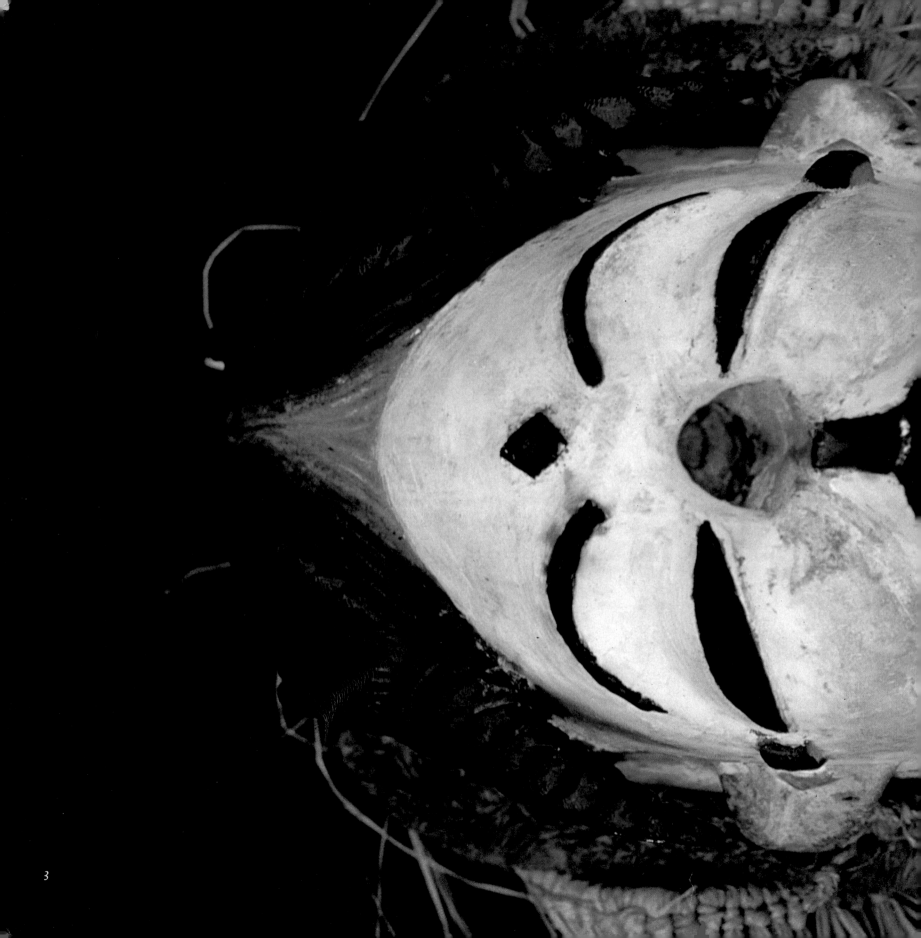

3

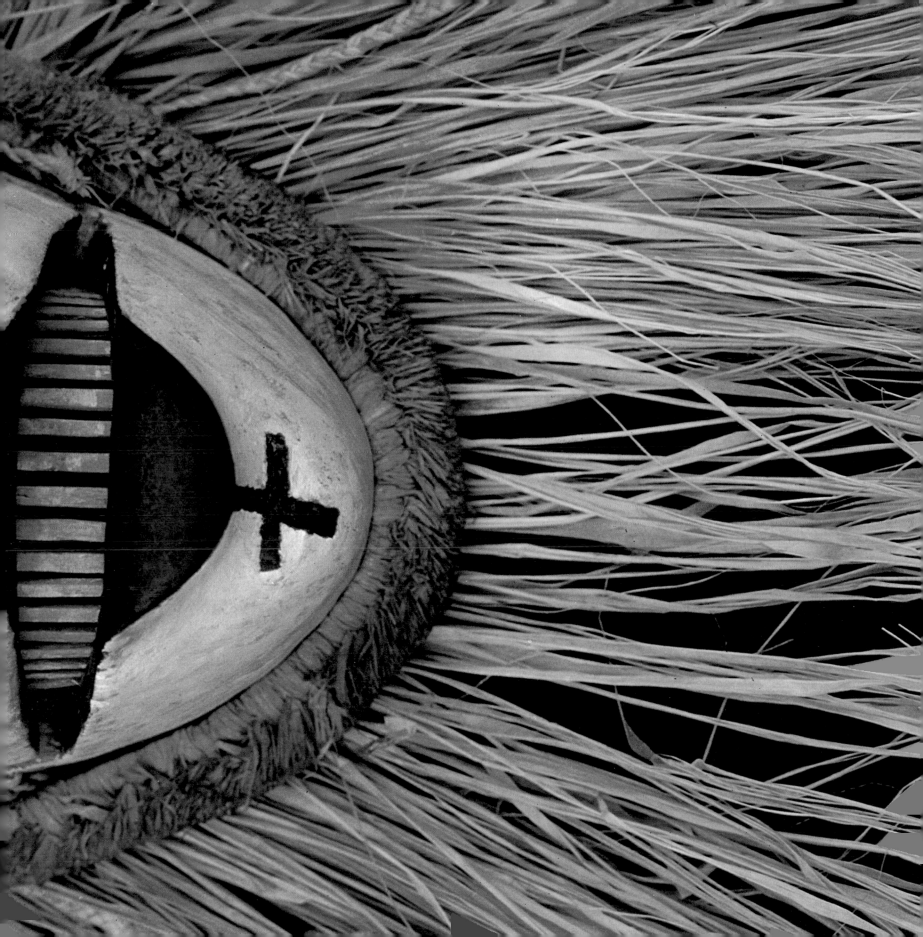

4

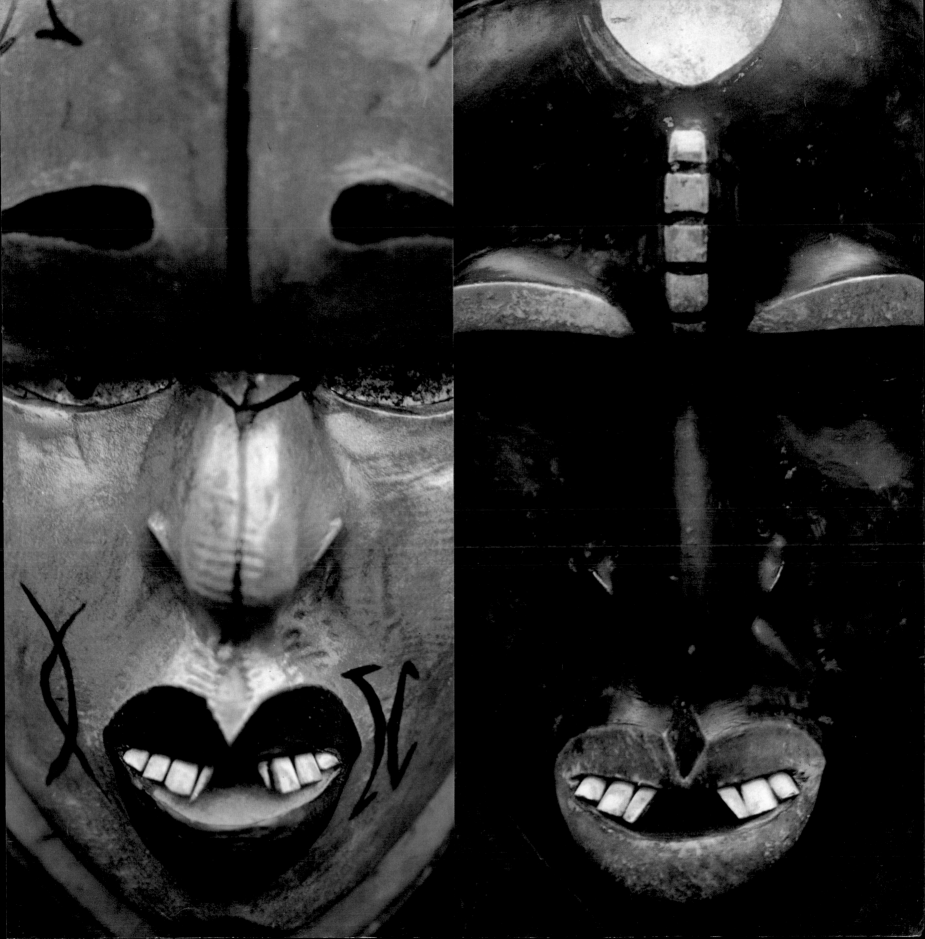

Plate 1 : A rare mask from the Igala tribe of Idah, the property of the **Ata** (King). Much of its powerful effect comes from the massed seeds of *Abrus precatorius.*

Plate 2 : This mask, from Ogboroke in the Igbira country, and the masquerade in which it is used are both called *osietengura,* literally 'he who makes the earth hot', or less literally 'someone who causes trouble' (compare the Lord of Misrule in European tradition). The surface is burned to a dark brown colour with a hot iron.

Plate 3 : The Ogoni (as the Ibo call them) or Kana (as they call themselves) live at the eastern corner of the Niger Delta, and are closely related in language and culture to the Ibibio. Their masks, most of them with movable lower jaws like this one, are chiefly used by acrobatic dancers.

Plate 4 : A water-spirit mask from the Ijebu Waterside around Epe, a Yoruba locality on the lagoon where there has been a fundamental penetration of Yoruba art by the art forms of the creek-living Ijo. It is called *imole ajoji* and is of the long and monstrous variety, horizontally worn, which combine human and animal and all sorts of other fantastic attributes. It was collected about 20 years ago.

Plate 5 : Skin-covered heads and masks are a special feature of the art of the Ejagham or Ekoi tribe of south-east Nigeria. The antelope skin, stained black for the male face, is stretched over the carved wood faces and pinned in with small wooden pegs. Such masks are used in the Ekkpe society. Note the '*nsibidi* writing' on the women's faces.

Plate 6 : Meko, on the border of Dahomey, is still a great centre for the carving of Gelede masks, which are used in pairs in dances for the propitiation of witches (that is to say of all womankind). Many of the masks, worn by men though generally representing women, have as

their superstructure images of modern life like sewing machines, aeroplanes and motor cars such as this Model-T Ford with prominent headlamps and klaxon. It was carved by Samuel Laroye before 1959.

Plate 7 : Part of a verandah in the Afin, or Palace, of the Alake of Abeokuta, the late Oba Samuel Gbadebo II. The carving at the extreme left appears to be by a good carver, Makinde, the son of Adugbologe, but the rest are by inferior and probably younger hands of the same family, whose work is mercifully obscured by the crude imported oil paints. Until about twenty years ago, there would have been many fine carvings by Adugbologe himself, such as two in a Swiss collection which probably came from here. In other parts of Yorubaland many fine masterpieces still survive in the palaces of the Obas.

Plate 8 : A priapic puppet, with movable parts, for the Udor Edem play, said to have been carved by Akpan Chuku of Utu Etim Ekpo in the Ibibio country of the South-East State.

Plate 9 : Two calabash vessels, the deeply carved one (right) being the lid of a vessel believed to have been collected by the explorer Baikie during his voyage up the Niger in the eighteen-forties. This style of carving seems to have become extinct during the past 120 years. The other is probably from the borders of Yoruba and Hausa country.

Plate 10 : The Ekkpe masquerade of the eastern Ibo of Bende and Aba districts – shared with the Ibibio and the Ejagham or Ekoi, among whom it seems to have originated – is based on two contrasting characters, the Elephant Spirit, standing for violence and ugliness, and the Maiden Spirit, who wears this headdress mask, and stands for all that is good, gentle and beautiful.

Bibliographical note

The art history of Nigeria from the earliest times to the present is treated in William Fagg, *Nigerian Images*, London and New York, 1963 (out of print, but available in some libraries; the French edition, *Merveilles de l'art Nigérien*, Paris, 1963, and the German edition, *Bildwerke aus Nigeria*, Munich, 1963, were, at last intelligence, still in print). Frank Willett's *African Sculpture*, London, 1971, is largely Nigeria-oriented, and so is excellent for seeing Nigeria in a wider context. Margaret Trowell's invaluable *African Design*, second edition, London, 1966, gives a compendious account of all the handicrafts of Africa, and should certainly be read by all who are interested by the present book.

Very valuable data on wood-carving from the standpoint of the artist are contained in Kevin Carroll's *Yoruba Religious Carving*, London, 1967, which also covers fully what is by far the most successful effort so far to arrest the demise of traditional wood-carving. Sylvia Leith-Ross has recently, in *Nigerian Pottery*, Ibadan, 1971, covered the whole field of pottery traditions as represented in the Pottery Museum at Jos (which was filled by her exertions). There is also a very good account of Yoruba *adire* dyeing in *Adire Cloth in Nigeria* edited by Jane Barbour and Doig Simmonds, Ibadan, 1971. The files of *Nigeria* magazine are a rich mine of information on tribal crafts, from its beginning as *The Nigerian Teacher* in the early thirties; the *Nigerian Field* may also be usefully searched. Many valuable articles may be found in the pages of *Man* from 1901 onwards, and in various other anthropological periodicals.